THE SCIENCE OF
NUTRITION

WHY WE NEED
FATS

By Molly Aloian

Crabtree Publishing Company

www.crabtreebooks.com

Crabtree Publishing Company

www.crabtreebooks.com

Author: Molly Aloian
Publishing plan research and development:
  Sean Charlebois, Reagan Miller
Editors: Sarah Eason, Nick Hunter, Lynn Peppas
Proofreaders: Robyn Hardyman, Kathy Middleton
Project coordinator: Kathy Middleton
Design: Calcium
Photo Research: Susannah Jayes
Print coordinator: Katherine Berti
Production coordinator and prepress technician:
  Ken Wright
Series consultant: Julie Negrin

Library and Archives Canada Cataloguing in Publication

Aloian, Molly
    Why we need fats / Molly Aloian.

(The science of nutrition)
Includes index.
Issued also in electronic format.
ISBN 978-0-7787-1687-7 (bound).--ISBN 978-0-7787-1694-5 (pbk.)

    1. Fatty acids in human nutrition--Juvenile literature.
2. Lipids in human nutrition--Juvenile literature. I. Title.
II. Series: Science of nutrition (St. Catharines, Ont.)

QP751.A46 2011   j612'.01577   C2011-900205-1

Library of Congress Cataloging-in-Publication Data

Aloian, Molly.
Why we need fats / Molly Aloian.
    p. cm. -- (The science of nutrition)
Includes index.
ISBN 978-0-7787-1694-5 (pbk. : alk. paper) -- ISBN 978-0-7787-1687-7 (reinforced library binding : alk. paper) -- ISBN 978-1-4271-9678-1 (electronic (pdf))
1. Fatty acids in human nutrition--Juvenile literature. 2. Lipids in human nutrition--Juvenile literature. I. Title. II. Series.

QP751.A39 2011
612.3'97--dc22

2010052740

Crabtree Publishing Company

www.crabtreebooks.com   1-800-387-7650

Printed in the U.S.A./022011/CJ20101228

Published in Canada
Crabtree Publishing
616 Welland Ave.
St. Catharines, Ontario
L2M 5V6

Published in the United States
Crabtree Publishing
PMB 59051
350 Fifth Avenue, 59th Floor
New York, New York 10118

Published in the United Kingdom
Crabtree Publishing
Maritime House
Basin Road North, Hove
BN41 1WR

Published in Australia
Crabtree Publishing
386 Mt. Alexander Rd.
Ascot Vale (Melbourne)
VIC 3032

CONTENTS

FOOD FOR FUEL

Eating a salad with a low-fat dressing gives you a balance of nutrients.

When you eat food–a peanut butter and jelly sandwich, for example–you might think you are just eating bread, peanut butter, and jelly, but you are eating much more than that. Hidden inside food are important **nutrients** that you need, not just to stay healthy, but to stay alive.

Food for energy

Your body needs energy for everything you do–even sleeping! Fats and **carbohydrates** provide you with energy. In a peanut butter and jelly sandwich, the bread is rich in mostly carbohydrate, the jelly is full of sugar, and the peanut butter contains fat. Try to get most of your energy from carbohydrates, because too many fatty foods will clog up your arteries, which is unhealthy for your heart.

The food pyramid shows healthy foods only. It does not include foods such as cookies and chips, which are high in salt, fat, or sugar.

Grains
Grains give you energy, but they also contain some protein and other nutrients.

Vegetables and fruits
You should eat a wide range from these two groups to get all the nutrients you need.

Oils and fats
These foods should not be overeaten.

Milk
This group of foods is rich in protein but can also be high in fat.

Meat and beans
These foods are rich in protein, although meats can also be high in fat.

You need nutrients

This book is about fats. There are two other main nutrients: **protein** and carbohydrates. Your body also needs tiny amounts of nutrients called vitamins and minerals. You have to eat enough—but not too much—of each kind of nutrient to stay healthy. Luckily, each type of nutrient is found in many different foods, so you can choose healthy food that you like.

The food pyramid divides healthy food into six different groups. Choosing foods from these groups will give you the nutrients you need.

WHAT ARE FATS?

Many people hear the word *fat* and think of something bad, but your body needs fat to be healthy. You would become very ill if you did not eat any fat at all.

Fat is good for you

It is important to eat fat because it contains vitamins and other important nutrients. It also supplies your body with the energy it needs.

One of three

Together with carbohydrates and proteins, fats are one of the three types of nutrients in foods that are used by the body for energy. Your body can store fats and use them later, or it can change fats into important chemicals.

Eating fat gives your body the energy it needs to be active.

Body Talk

Fats are one of the main nutrients that people need to survive. The fatty tissues in your body protect your organs and make up the **membranes** surrounding your cells.

Did you know?

Carbohydrates, fats, proteins, and water are called macronutrients because your body needs them in large amounts. The word *macro* means "large." Your body needs micronutrients such as vitamins and minerals in smaller amounts. The word *micro* means "small."

Fat for fuel

Fat is the most efficient source of energy the body can use. Every gram of fat gives your body nine **calories** of energy. Carbohydrates and proteins only provide four calories of energy per gram. However, you need to be active to burn off the extra energy from fat, or your body stores it and you will become overweight.

Solid or liquid

Scientists call fatty substances **lipids**. There are many different kinds of fats. Depending on their chemical structure, fats can be either solid or liquid at room temperature. Fats are lipids that are solid at room temperature. Liquid lipids are usually called oils. All lipids have a slick, greasy feel when you rub them between your fingers.

At room temperature, butter is a solid fat. Heating solid butter in a frying pan turns it into a liquid.

What is fat made from?

There are different kinds of fats, but they all contain two kinds of chemicals. These chemicals are called **fatty acids** and **glycerol**. They are made up of carbon, hydrogen, and oxygen.

Essential elements

Carbon, hydrogen, and oxygen are chemical elements. These substances are made up of just one kind of **atom**. The carbon, hydrogen, and oxygen in fatty acids and glycerol join together in ways that allow fats to store energy.

Most of the foods we eat—even vegetables such as carrots—contain fat.

Even a salad is not completely "fat free"!

Did you know?

Even foods that you might think are fat free, such as carrots, lettuce, and potatoes, contain tiny amounts of fat. This shows how important fats are for life.

Body Talk

Your body stores fat under the surface of your skin, especially around your buttocks, giving you a nice, natural cushion to sit on!

Chains of fatty acids

A fatty acid is a chain of carbon atoms with hydrogen atoms stuck onto it. Fatty acids are found in animal and plant fat. Some chains of fatty acids have only a few carbon atoms. Others have 20 carbon atoms or more. Liquid fats, such as oils, contain short chains of carbon atoms. Fatty acids with long chains of carbon atoms are usually solid fats.

Fatty acids are made up of carbon atoms (C), hydrogen atoms (H), and oxygen (O).

Glycerides

Scientists use the word *glyceride* to describe fat. A glyceride is made up of glycerol and one or more fatty acids. Glycerol has three places where the fatty acids can attach.

If there is one fatty acid on the glycerol, the fat is a monoglyceride. *Mono* is the Latin word for "one." If the fat has two fatty acids on the glycerol, it is called a diglyceride. *Di* means "two." If a fat has three fatty acids on the glycerol it is called a triglyceride. *Tri* means "three."

Carbon bonds

Some fatty acids have more hydrogen atoms connected to the carbon chain than other fatty acids. Connections between the atoms are called bonds. Each carbon atom can form four bonds with other atoms.

Saturated fats

In some fatty acids, most of the carbon atoms form two bonds with two other carbon atoms in the chain and two bonds with two hydrogen atoms. These fatty acids make saturated fats because the carbon atoms are full, or "saturated." This means that each carbon atom forms bonds with as many different carbon and hydrogen atoms as possible.

Unsaturated fats

In an unsaturated fatty acid, a carbon atom can form a double bond with the neighboring carbon atom in the chain and two bonds with other carbon or hydrogen atoms. Monounsaturated fatty acids contain only one carbon double bond. (Remember, *mono* means "one.") Polyunsaturated fatty acid has more than one carbon double bond in the fatty acid.

Unsaturated fat contains fewer carbon-hydrogen bonds than saturated fat with the same number of carbon atoms. Fewer bonds means less energy in the fat, so unsaturated fats provide less energy than saturated fats.

The fat from pigs and other animals is saturated fat. The fat you see on a slice of bacon is unhealthy fat.

Unsalted peanuts are a tasty snack and a healthy source of unsaturated fats.

I love potato chips, but they are usually full of unhealthy saturated fats.

Trans fats

Trans fats are made by heating liquid vegetable oils in hydrogen gas. This process is called **hydrogenation**, and it prevents vegetable oils from spoiling. Hydrogenated vegetable oils can also withstand being heated again and again without breaking down, which makes them ideal for frying fast foods.

Trans fats are unhealthy fats because the hydrogenation adds energy to the fat. They are found in **processed** foods. Be sure to read labels and avoid foods that have "partially hydrogenated oils" in the list of ingredients.

Body Talk

Fats from plants, including corn, peanut, and olive oils, contain unsaturated fat. These fats are healthy fats. Fats from animals, such as butter and bacon fat, contain saturated fat. Saturated fats are unhealthy and linked to a number of medical problems, including heart disease and certain types of cancer.

11

WHERE DO WE GET FATS?

Foods that have unhealthy fats often have a smooth, rich, and pleasant taste. Eating foods that contain lots of unhealthy fats is dangerous, especially when there are many other foods that contain unsaturated fats that are good for you.

Ice cream may taste delicious, but it is full of unhealthy saturated fat.

You only need a little saturated fat

You get saturated fats mainly from meat, seafood, poultry with skin, and whole-milk dairy products such as cheese, milk, and ice cream. A few plant foods are also high in saturated fats, including coconut and coconut oil, palm oil, and palm kernel oil. Your body makes most of the saturated fat you need, so you only need to get a little of this fat from your food. It is best to get saturated fats from nuts, seeds, and oils, with just a little from animal food.

Did you know?

In the 1960s, scientists found that people in the United States got about 45 percent of their calories from fatty foods. At the time, about 13 percent of the population was **obese** and one percent had **diabetes**. Today, Americans eat less fat, getting about 33 percent of calories from fats and oils. But 34 percent of the population is obese and eight percent have diabetes.

Most people have type 2 diabetes. Type 2 occurs, not only because of the total amount of fat consumed, but because of the type of fat consumed. Bad fats, such as trans fats and saturated fats, increase the risk of developing diabetes and other diseases.

Finding trans fat

There are often a lot of trans fats in cakes and other baked goods, processed foods, snack foods, and margarines. Fries and other fried foods prepared in fast-food restaurants also contain trans fat.

Fries are full of trans fats. Try a baked potato for a healthier option.

Not so healthy...

For years margarine was promoted as a healthy alternative to butter. Since margarine was made from unsaturated vegetable oils, most people assumed it would be healthier than butter, which was known to contain a lot of cholesterol and saturated fat. That assumption turned out to be wrong.

Worse than butter!

Research shows that some forms of margarine made with partially hydrogenated oils—specifically hard, stick margarines—are worse for the heart than butter. This is because they contain large amounts of trans fats from hydrogenated vegetable oils.

Body Talk

According to one study, women who ate four teaspoons (20 ml) of stick margarine a day had a 50 percent greater risk of heart disease than women who ate margarine only rarely.

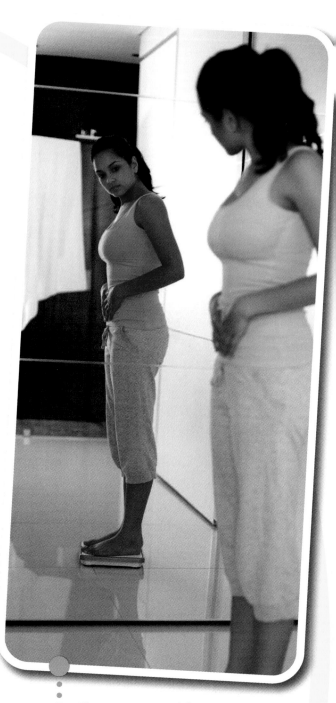

If you are watching your weight, it is important to keep an eye on the type of fat you are eating.

Try this...

It is important to figure out how many of the calories you are consuming come from fat. But food labels do not always show the percentage of fat in a food. It is easy to calculate though. Divide the number of calories from fat by the number of total calories and multiply by 100:

$$\frac{\text{Calories from fat}}{\text{Total calories}} \times 100 = \text{percent of fat}$$

For example, if a 300-calorie food has 60 calories from fat, you divide 60 by 300 and then multiply by 100. The result shows that particular food gets 20 percent of its calories from fat:

$$\frac{60}{300} \times 100 = 20\%$$

Vegetable oil is best

So which is worse: butter or margarine? Whenever possible, try to eat a liquid vegetable oil because it is full of healthy unsaturated fats. You and your family can try dipping bread in olive oil instead of spreading it with butter or margarine. If you want to use margarine, choose one that is free of unhealthy trans fats.

Try olive oil on your bread as a healthy alternative to butter.

My mom usually pours olive oil on our salads. It tastes great.

Where can we find healthy fats?

Monounsaturated fats and polyunsaturated fats are healthy fats. Avocados, canola, olive oil, peanuts, nuts such as almonds, hazelnuts, and pecans, and seeds such as pumpkin seeds and sesame seeds are good sources of monounsaturated fats. Foods that contain polyunsaturated fats include sunflower, corn, and soybeans, as well as walnuts and flax seeds. Some fish contain healthy omega-3 fatty acids.

Fantastic fruit

The avocado is an excellent source of healthy unsaturated fats. This fruit is packed with nearly 20 essential nutrients, including minerals such as potassium, fiber, and vitamins. Avocados also act as a "nutrient booster," helping the body to absorb more fat-soluble nutrients in foods that are eaten with the fruit.

Did you know?

Some people believe that if they start working out they turn their fat into muscle or that, if they stop working out, their muscle will turn into fat. Neither is true. Each tissue is distinctly different. You can gain or lose muscle, and you can gain or lose more body fat, but they do not convert into each other.

Slice an avocado and add it to a salad for a healthy hit of unsaturated fat.

The healthy choice

Most people do not get enough healthy fats each day. Some nutritionists estimate that ten to 25 percent of calories should come from monounsaturated fats, and eight to ten percent of calories should come from polyunsaturated fats. A good rule of thumb is to choose unsaturated fats over saturated whenever possible.

Who is counting?

Food experts think that an average adult man should eat no more than one ounce (30 g) of saturated fat a day. And it can quickly add up. Just one take-out burger from a popular fast-food restaurant contains exactly that amount of saturated fat—even without a side order of fries. It is time to watch what you are eating.

Body Talk

Most medical experts say that children and teens between the ages of four and 18 should get between 25 percent and 35 percent of their daily calories from fat.

No matter how hard you try, you cannot turn fat into muscle!

Young, active people need to eat more healthy fat to fuel their bodies and help them grow.

HOW MUCH FAT DO WE NEED?

In poor countries, many people struggle to get all the nutrients they need, including fat.

You might be surprised to discover that the total amount of fat you eat, whether that total is high or low, is not actually that closely linked to how healthy you are. What really matters is the type of fat you eat.

Getting low

Many people think that a low-fat, low-cholesterol diet is the best way to lose weight and stop health problems such as heart disease. Eating low-fat foods may make a difference for certain people, but not everyone can control their weight or health by eating low-fat foods.

Many low-fat products contain more sugar and other additives to make up for the loss in flavor from the fat. These extra ingredients often make the product less healthy than if the original fat was just left in it. It is best to eat natural foods that do not contain extra sugars and additives.

Eating high-fat foods such as cookies causes health problems such as heart disease.

Did you know?

October 16th is World Food Day. This is an international event that highlights the problems of hunger and increases awareness about the type of foods people are eating. On World Food Day, people may discuss issues such as why there is not enough food in some countries or why people are eating too much trans fat in their food. Talking about these problems makes a big difference to people's health.

Losing out

People following low-fat diets may face one big problem. In their attempts to limit or stop eating any fat, they might also stop eating healthy fats that are good for the heart. In place of fats, many of these people might start eating foods that are full of easily digested carbohydrates. They might also eat fat-free products that replace healthy fats with sugar and refined carbohydrates, which are unhealthy.

Not all food is good food

In poor countries, many people do not have enough food and struggle to get all the nutrients they need. It is the opposite problem in the West. People have enough food, but it is unhealthy food that contains too much bad fat.

Too much trans fat and saturated fat can be dangerous. Both of these fats are linked to heart disease, obesity, certain cancers, and other health problems. People are slowly becoming more aware of these dangers and making healthy food choices to avoid trans and saturated fats.

Body Talk

Studies have shown that women with diets high in animal fat had up to a 50 percent higher risk of developing breast cancer than women who ate less animal fat. Red meat and high-fat dairy products may contain other substances, such as hormones, that also increase the risk of breast cancer.

Blood block

Eating too much saturated fats increases your body's cholesterol level. Saturated fats and cholesterol can build up on the inner walls of blood vessels. This condition is called atherosclerosis. When the heart's arteries become clogged with cholesterol and fats, blood flow can be restricted or totally blocked. This can cause severe chest pains and heart attacks.

Eating too much red meat, such as beef from cows, increases your risk of developing health problems.

Gaining weight

Eating too much fat can make your body too fat. Being overweight can increase blood pressure, place extra strain on your heart, and make it more difficult for you to stay active and physically fit. All of these factors can badly affect your overall health.

Burgers and other fast foods should be kept to an occasional treat.

Did you know?

Approximately 49 percent of every food dollar in the United States is spent on food eaten outside the home, including take-out meals. Between the 1970s and the mid-1990s, restaurant dining increased from 18 percent to 32 percent of the total caloric intake of Americans.

Cutting back

Research has shown that a lack of exercise and being overweight can lead to insulin resistance. Eating a lot of processed carbohydrates can also cause insulin resistance. Cutting back on refined grains and eating more whole grains can help prevent and improve insulin resistance. Eating whole grains can also help to prevent type 2 diabetes, heart disease, certain cancers, and other health problems.

IT'S ON THE LABEL

You can get important information from the labels on food packaging. They can give you an idea about what the food contains, how much is in a serving, and how many calories it contains. Take a look at a label and compare two food groups. Which food has more fiber? Which one has more fat? Which one has more calories per serving?

Both the U.S. and Canadian governments require that packaged foods have nutrition labels. Reading food labels is a great way to learn more about the ingredients and nutrients in the foods that you are eating.

It is important to read the labels on food packaging to know what you are eating.

Nutrition Facts

Serving Size 1/6 package (60g)
Servings Per Container 6

Amount Per Serving	Mix	Prepared
Calories	260	360
Calories from Fat	80	150
	% Daily Value*	
Total Fat 9g*	14%	26%
Saturated Fat 3.5g	18%	30%
Cholesterol 0mg	0%	1%
Sodium 360mg	15%	20%
Total Carbohydrate 46g	15%	16%
Dietary Fiber 1g	4%	4%
Sugars 28g		
Protein 2g		
Vitamin A	0%	10%
	0%	0%

Food packaging must clearly show the fat content of the food it contains.

Start reading

Food labels contain specific information about serving size, total calories, calories from fat, a list of ingredients, and other important information. When you are reading a food label, keep in mind that although your body needs some fat, salt, and sugar, these nutrients should be eaten in small amounts. They might make foods taste better, but they do not make the foods healthier for you.

A balanced diet

Food labels try to show how one serving of the packaged food fits into a daily balanced diet. For example, for a 2,000-calorie-per-day diet, some health experts suggest that approximately 300–400 of these calories should come from fat.

Did you know?

The Percent Daily Value is the percentage of the suggested daily amount of a nutrient in a food serving based on a 2,000-calorie diet. Over the course of one day, the Percent Daily Values of each nutrient in foods you eat should add up to 100 percent.

Active, young children need more calories from their food than older people because they are still growing.

Body Talk

Puberty in children is triggered by a hormone produced by body fat. For girls, eating too much animal fat and being obese as a child can lead to **puberty** starting earlier than usual. Earlier maturity of the body can increase the risk of breast cancer later in life.

Math comes in handy when you are reading the labels on food.

Biggest to smallest

The list of ingredients in a food is listed on the food label in order from the greatest to the least percentage by weight. For example, the first ingredient on a box of crackers might be flour. This means that in the crackers, flour makes up most of the cracker's weight.

More or less

When you are reading food labels, keep in mind that a younger person's diet might include more or less than 2,000 calories per day, based on the person's age, whether they are a boy or girl, and how active they are on a daily basis. Young people may need more or less of certain nutrients, such as calcium, protein, and iron.

Servings per package

The nutrition label should also tell you how many servings are contained in that package of food. If there are 15 servings in a box of cookies and each serving is two cookies, you have enough for all 30 kids in your class to have one cookie each.

Serving size

The nutrition label always lists a serving size, which is an amount of food, such as one cup (240 ml) of cereal, two cookies, or five pretzels. The nutrition label tells you how many nutrients are in that amount of food. Serving sizes also help people understand and keep track of how much food and how many calories they are eating.

Did you know?

Most nutrients are measured in grams, also written as "g." Some nutrients are measured in milligrams, or mg. Milligrams are very tiny—there are 1,000 milligrams in one gram.

Fifteen cookies in a package provides 15 servings of food. You should eat just one or two servings—not the whole package!

What does it all mean?

Low fat, reduced fat, light, and fat free are common terms you will see on food packaging in North America. Governments have strict rules about how food manufacturers use these phrases. By law, fat-free foods can contain up to 0.02 ounces (0.5 g) of fat per serving. Low-fat foods can have 0.1 ounces (3 g) of fat or less per serving. For foods marked "reduced fat" and "light" (or "lite"), it is a little bit harder to understand.

I thought "light" meant low-fat—until I checked the label!

Did you know?

Sometimes when you feel hungry you are really feeling thirsty. Try a glass of water instead of a snack. It will fill you up and make you more alert. Everyone should drink at least eight large glasses of water every day.

Peanut butter sandwiches are a tasty snack, but they contain a lot of fat.

Total Fat 0g

Saturated Fat

Chol

Food labels are the best way to check the nutritional content of your food.

Light and reduced

Light (or "lite") and reduced-fat foods may still be high in fat. The requirement for a food to be labeled light (or "lite") is that it must contain 50 percent less fat or one-third fewer calories per serving than the regular version of that food.

Foods labeled reduced fat must contain 25 percent less fat per serving than the regular version. However, if the regular version of a particular food was high in fat to begin with, 25 percent to 50 percent less fat may not lower the fat content

Body Talk

The feeling of hunger is your body's physical need for food. A cone-shaped part of your brain called the hypothalamus makes you feel hungry when you need food. It also makes you feel thirsty when your body needs water.

enough to make it a smart food choice. For example, the original version of a brand of peanut butter contains 0.6 ounces (17 g) of fat per serving. The reduced-fat version contains 0.4 ounces (12 g), but that is still a lot of fat in a single serving!

27

NO FEAR OF FAT

Your body needs fat to function properly. Fats provide your body with the energy it needs for physical activity. Fats have more than twice the energy in the form of calories than both protein and carbohydrates.

Fat protects you

You need fat because it gives your body its shape and protects it. If you look in the mirror, you will be able to see fatty tissues on your hips, thighs, buttocks, and belly. This fat is cushioning your skin and helps to protect your organs and bones if you fall or are injured. Fat acts like an insulation blanket that prevents your body from losing heat. This visible fat is like a reserve source of energy. You can also thank fat for your healthy skin and shiny hair.

> *I thought I was getting fat, but my mom said all girls get curves when they go through puberty.*

Your body starts to use fat as fuel when you exercise. The layer of fat under your skin also keeps your body warm.

Body Talk

People who do not have enough fat in their diets can suffer from dry skin, hair loss, and bruising. They are more likely to become sick, too.

Fat is essential for healthy skin and hair.

Women also need fat around their hips and tummy to be able to have healthy pregnancies and children.

Fats work with vitamins

Fats are also needed to absorb certain vitamins that are essential for proper growth. Vitamins A, D, E, and K are fat soluble, which means they can only be absorbed if there is fat in your diet. These vitamins are absorbed in the small **intestine**.

Did you know?

No offense, but you have a really fat head! Approximately two-thirds of your brain is made up of fats.

The fatty acids from food are used by your brain to make the cells that help you solve difficult math problems.

Did you know?

Myelin, the protective sheath that covers neurons, is composed of 30 percent protein and 70 percent fat.

Fats help you learn

Your brain cells require very specialized fats—the same ones that helped form the brains of people from thousands of years ago and enabled them to learn and evolve at such a fast rate. As you read this sentence, these same fats are now being incorporated into the very structure of your own brain.

Building up the brain

The membranes of **neurons** are made up of a thin, double layer of fatty acid **molecules**. Neurons are special cells that send messages around the body. When your body digests the fat in your food, it is broken down into fatty-acid molecules of various lengths. Your brain uses the fatty acid chains to build the membranes around body cells. Fatty acids are important building blocks for a healthy brain.

Body Talk

Omega-3 fats are the building blocks of bones— the fatty acids within the fats help hold minerals in bone and increase the formation of new bone.

Friendly fats

Omega-3 fatty acids are heart friendly. They are most commonly found in fatty fish such as salmon and sardines. Omega-3 fats make tiny particles in blood, called platelets, less sticky. This reduces the chance that they will clump together to form blood **clots**. Blood clots can block a blood vessel and trigger a heart attack. The American Heart Association recommends eating fish at least twice a week because these omega-3 fats also lower bad cholesterol levels.

Eating oily fish really does boost your brain power.

DIGESTING FATS

Your **digestive system** is all the parts of your body that work together to change the food you eat into particles that are small enough for your cells to absorb. It takes your body longer to digest fats than it does to digest carbohydrates or proteins.

Getting ready

When you chew your food, you are helping to soften the fats in the food and preparing them for digestion. The warmth from your body also helps to soften fats. Your **esophagus** moves food from the mouth into the stomach. Only a small amount of fat is digested by gastric juices in the stomach. The fat from food moves from your stomach into the small intestine.

Digestion begins as soon as food enters your mouth.

Small intestine

In the small intestine, large fat molecules mix with a digestive chemical called bile. Bile is made in your liver and stored in your gallbladder until it is needed for digestion. Bile breaks up fats into smaller molecules so **enzymes** can digest them. Digestive juices from the **pancreas** digest large molecules of fats.

esophagus

liver

stomach

pancreas

small intestine

Food passes down the esophagus into the stomach, then on to the small intestine. The liver and pancreas produce digestive enzymes that break down food into smaller molecules.

Body Talk

The small intestine is about 22 feet (7 m) long and is between 1 and 1.5 inches (2.5 and 3.8 cm) wide. The large intestine is between the small intestine and the **rectum**. It is approximately twice as large in diameter as the small intestine. The large intestine is U-shaped and is usually between 5 and 6 feet (1.5 and 1.8 m) long.

Into the blood stream

The nutrients from the digested food pass through the wall of your small intestine and into the bloodstream. Your blood then delivers these nutrients to all the cells in your body.

Did you know?

Fat is digested more slowly than carbohydrates or proteins. As a result, you feel full longer after eating a high-fat meal.

The role of bile

In the small intestine, bile acts like an **emulsifier**. If you stir a mixture of fruit juice and water, the two liquids will completely mix with each other. They dissolve in each other. But some liquids do not mix with each other. Take oil and water. Mix them together and the oil forms tiny droplets on the surface of the water. When this happens, the mixture is called an emulsion.

An emulsifier is a substance that helps two substances mix when they would normally try to stay apart—such as oil and water. Bile is an emulsifier. Your liver produces bile to help the body absorb fat, so that other substances can start to break it down.

Research has shown that eating foods rich in omega-3 fatty acids can help people who suffer from depression.

Your body works hard to break down the fat in fast foods such as burgers.

Body Talk

Some health experts think people should increase their intake of healthy omega-3 fatty acids. You need these for body processes such as the clotting of blood and the building of cell membranes in the brain. Foods that are rich in omega-3 fatty acids include oily fish such as anchovies, herring, mackerel, salmon, and sardines.

Breaking down fats

Lipase is a chemical that the body uses to digest the fats in food. It breaks down large fat molecules into smaller fats and fatty acids. These are more easily absorbed through the wall of the intestine and into the blood. Most of the lipase in your body is made in the pancreas, but smaller amounts are also produced in the mouth and stomach. Most people produce enough lipase to digest fat. But people with celiac disease (an **intolerance** to a protein called gluten in wheat) may not have enough lipase to get the nutrition they need from their food.

35

BEING FAT

When people say "you are what you eat," they might be telling the truth, especially when talking about fat. You only use up the fat you need to give you the energy to move around and keep warm. If you eat more fat, your body stores it for later. As you eat more and more fat without burning it away, you will become overweight.

It is important to remember that everyone needs some body fat. Being overweight is unhealthy, but so is having too little body fat.

Did you know?

People are obese when they have a body mass index (BMI) of 30 or more. The BMI is the comparison of a person's weight to their height. It is a good indication of how overweight a person really is.

A weighty problem

Being overweight is a health issue. Everyone needs to store a little fat on their bodies. But people who overeat and do not get enough exercise start to store too much fat. Then they become obese. Today, more than 30 percent of adults and 17 percent of children in the United States and more than 20 percent of adults and about ten percent of children in Canada are obese. Health problems related to obesity cost billions of dollars in healthcare every year.

Try this...

What you need:
- desk lamp
- brown paper bag
- ruler
- scissors
- pen
- eyedropper
- vegetable oil
- paper towel
- carrot, mayonnaise, potato chip, bagel, water, and grape juice

Instructions:

1. Draw eight 2-inch (5 cm) squares on the paper bag and cut them out. Take two of the squares as the control samples. Label one square "No Oil" and the other "Oil."

2. Put a drop of vegetable oil in the center of the paper marked "Oil." Rub the oil across the paper with your finger.

3. Rub each food or drink sample on each of the remaining paper squares. Label each one and leave them to dry.

4. Hold the "No Oil" and "Oil" squares up to a light. See how much more light shines through the "Oil" paper? Compare each of the food squares to the "Oil" and "No Oil" control squares.

What just happened:

If the sample made the paper more see-through, it contained more fat.

CHOLESTEROL

Cholesterol is another kind of fat. It is found in nearly every tissue in your body. It is a wax-like substance that is made in your liver, and it does many important jobs. Cholesterol also comes from food. Your body needs cholesterol to carry out its daily tasks, but you only need a small amount of cholesterol from the food you eat.

Cholesterol in the blood

Fat and cholesterol cannot dissolve in water or blood. Your body carries fat and cholesterol as tiny particles called **lipoproteins**. Although lipoproteins can carry fat, they also mix with blood. In this way, blood can carry fat around the body. Some lipoproteins are big and fluffy. These are called low-density lipoproteins (LDL). Others are small and dense, or firm. These are called high-density lipoproteins (HDL).

Good and bad

HDL cholesterol is a good type of cholesterol. HDL cholesterol helps clear the LDL cholesterol out of the blood and reduces the risk of developing heart disease. LDL cholesterol is a bad type of cholesterol. This is the cholesterol that clogs blood vessels, increasing your risk of heart disease.

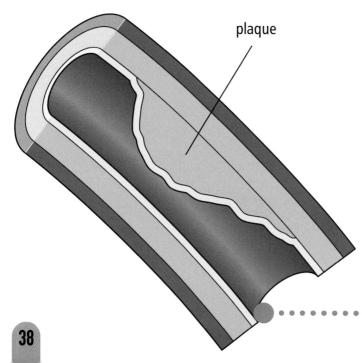

plaque

Too much cholesterol in the body causes a build up of fat, called plaque, in the arteries.

Did you know?

Your body makes approximately 1,000 milligrams of cholesterol a day. This is all the cholesterol your body needs. But cholesterol is found in many different foods, so it is hard to avoid eating extra cholesterol. Cholesterol contains no calories, and it provides your body with no energy.

Body Talk

When your body has too much cholesterol, it can build up in the walls of blood vessels called arteries, making it harder for blood to flow. If the coronary arteries, which provide blood to the heart, become narrow, blood flow can slow down or stop. This can cause chest pain and shortness of breath. It can even lead to a heart attack.

I found out that meat, eggs, and dairy foods contain cholesterol.

Milk contains a lot of vitamins and calcium, which can help keep your bones strong and healthy. But it also contains a lot of fat, which boosts your body's cholesterol level.

Cholesterol in food

Many foods contain cholesterol. There are about 213 milligrams of cholesterol in a medium-sized egg. A three-ounce (85 g) portion of lean red meat or skinless chicken contains about 90 milligrams of cholesterol. A three-ounce (85 g) portion of fish contains about 50 milligrams of cholesterol.

Plant it

Other foods that contain cholesterol include animal organs such as liver and kidney, dairy products such as milk and heavy cream, and seafood such as shrimps and lobster. Most plant foods including breakfast cereals, fruits, whole grains, vegetables, nuts, and seeds do not contain cholesterol.

Body Talk

Most of the cholesterol-rich foods that people eat come from animal products such as meat and milk. Eating a plant-based diet is healthiest for your body. Be sure to eat plenty of fruits, vegetables, whole grains, and healthy fats such as olive oil and canola oil. Your body can better use these plant-based foods, and they are healthy choices.

Diabetes and children

Recent studies have shown that children between the ages of eight and ten years old are being diagnosed with type 2 diabetes, high cholesterol, and high blood pressure at an alarming rate. Food experts think that children are eating too much processed food, which contains a lot of saturated fat. Not getting enough exercise is also contributing to the problem.

Egg yolks are a particularly rich source of cholesterol.

It is not all bad

You might be worried about eating too much cholesterol and fatty food, but your body needs some fat. Extremely low-fat diets may not contain enough of the omega-3 and omega-6 essential fatty acids your body needs. Eating a balanced diet with all the different nutrients is the best way to stay healthy and look after your body.

Did you know?

The word *cholesterol* comes from the Greek words *chole*, which means "bile," and *stereos*, which means "solid or stiff."

Shrimps have a high cholesterol content, but they are low in saturated fat, which raises cholesterol levels in the body.

My friend ate too much cholesterol, and now he has diabetes. He is only nine years old.

SPECIAL DIETS

There are many different reasons why people need more or less fat in their diet.

Different people need different amounts of nutrients in their food. If you play a lot of sports, for example, you will need extra carbohydrates, protein, and fat to get the energy you need to make the tackle or win the race. Your body will lose valuable vitamins and minerals through your sweat and urine, so you will need a nutrient boost after strenuous exercise.

Babies and young children need more fat than adults because their bodies are still growing.

Growing up

Young children need less food than adults, but they need more fat as a percentage of their diet to grow and develop into healthy adults. Fat provides more energy than carbohydrates and protein, so it is important for children to get enough fat from their food. Food experts recommend that fat should make up around 30 to 35 percent of a child's total calorie intake.

Did you know?

Food experts think that if North Americans replaced all the unhealthy trans fats in their diets with healthy polyunsaturated fats from vegetables, diabetes could be reduced by up to 40 percent.

A glass of milk is good for children because their growing bodies need extra fat.

Growing older

As you grow older, your body changes. You still need fat, but not too much. Adults should eat more carbohydrates to get the energy they need. Fat should only make up about 20 percent of the total calorie intake.

Pregnancy

Women need extra nutrients when they are pregnant. A woman's body goes through many changes when she is pregnant. Extra nutrients are needed to help the fetus inside her develop into a healthy baby, as well as support her own body.

Body Talk

Some people cannot eat hydrogenated fats. They have a food allergy. The body reacts to the fat thinking it is harmful. Symptoms include headaches, feeling sick, hot flushes, indigestion, and other health problems, such as hayfever and eczema. The only way to prevent the symptoms is to avoid any foods that contain hydrogenated fats.

FOOD FACTS AND STATS

A balanced diet needs to contain a proper mix of carbohydrates, fat, and protein. A healthy low-fat diet includes a lot of whole grains, beans, fruits, and vegetables. You also need small amounts of healthy sources of fat including nuts, seeds, and vegetable oils such as olive oil, flaxseed oil, and soybean oil. Fish such as salmon, herring, and mackerel are also good sources of healthy fat.

Healthy and low in fat

Follow these tips to make healthy choices about the food you eat:

- Try to cut out trans fats from partially hydrogenated oils. Check food labels for trans fats and be sure to avoid fried fast foods.

- Limit your intake of saturated fats by cutting back on red meat and full-fat dairy foods. Try replacing red meat with beans, nuts, poultry, and fish whenever possible. Switch from whole milk and other full-fat dairy foods to low-fat versions.

- In place of butter, try to use liquid vegetable oils rich in polyunsaturated and monounsaturated fats in cooking and at the dinner table.

- Eat one or more good sources of omega-3 fats every day—fish, walnuts, canola or soybean oil, ground flax seeds, or flaxseed oil.

Recommended daily amounts of fats for adults and children aged 4 and over

Total fat	2.3 oz (65 g)
Saturated fatty acids	0.7 oz (20 g)
Cholesterol	300 mg

Recommended daily amounts of different kinds of food for children aged 9 to 13

Grains	5 oz (140 g) (girls) 6 oz (170 g) (boys)
Vegetables	2 cups (475 ml) (girls) 2.5 cups (600 ml) (boys)
Fruit	1.5 cups (350 ml)
Milk	3 cups (700 ml)
Meat and beans	5 oz (140 g)
Oils	5 teaspoons (25ml)

Comparing calories

Energy in food is measured in calories. This is what one ounce (28 g) gives:

Carbohydrate	105 calories
Protein	112 calories
Fat	252 calories

Food manufacturers must show information about the fat content of food on the food labels. They must show the following information:

- total calories
- calories from saturated fat
- saturated fat
- monounsaturated fat
- calories from fat
- total fat
- polyunsaturated fat
- cholesterol

GLOSSARY

atom Smallest part of an element that can exist alone

calorie Unit measuring the amount of energy a food will produce

carbohydrate Sugar or starch that is the main source of energy

clot A lump created when liquid thickens and sticks together

diabetes Disease in which the body lacks insulin

digestive system Part of the body that turns food into elements your body needs

emulsifier Any substance that helps to break down fat

enzyme Protein that helps to break down food in your system

esophagus Tube that runs from your throat to your stomach

fatty acid A molecule in fat

glycerol Alcohol that forms the backbone of fatty acids in fats

hydrogenation Chemical process that adds hydrogen atoms to liquid fats to turn them into solid fats

intestine Long tube in the body through which food passes after leaving the stomach

intolerance Unable to eat certain foods that the body reacts badly to

lipid Any kind of fat in your body

lipoprotein Chemical found in the bloodstream that consists of simple proteins bound to fat

membrane Thin layer of tissue

molecule Smallest part of a substance

nutrient Healthy source of nourishment

obese Having an abnormally high, unhealthy amount of body fat

pancreas Gland behind the stomach

process To change or prepare food using several ingredients and other substances such as salt and chemicals

protein One of the main nutrients

puberty Phase of life when children's bodies change to become adults

rectum Lowest part of your bowels

saliva Watery mixture in the mouth

FURTHER READING

Further Reading

Sayer, Dr. Melissa, *Too Fat? Too Thin? The Healthy Eating Guidebook*. Crabtree Publishing, 2009.

Doeden, Matt, *Eat Right*, Lerner, 2009.

Gardner, Robert, *Health Science Projects about Nutrition*. Enslow Publishers, 2002.

Powell, Jillian. *Fats for a Healthy Body*. Heinemann-Raintree, 2009.

Sohn, Emily, and Sarah Webb. *Food and Nutrition*. Chelsea Clubhouse, 2006.

Internet

Learning about Fats and Cholesterol
www.hsph.harvard.edu/nutritionsource/
  what-should-you-eat/
  fats-and-cholesterol/index.html

Your Digestive System
http://kidshealth.org/kid/htbw/
  digestive_system.html

Try this...

Keep a food journal. Write down everything you eat for an entire week. How much fat did you eat? Were they healthy or unhealthy fats? Which foods did they come from?

INDEX